"Jentezen Franklin reveals the strategic influence wise and discerning men and women can have in the lives of those around them. Allow *Right People, Right Place, Right Plan* to alter your perspective and speak to your heart."

—*Joyce Meyer*
Best-selling author and Bible teacher

"Jentezen Franklin, in this exciting and life changing book, reveals how men and women of discernment forever change the lives of people in their circles of influence. If you read one book this year, make it *Right People, Right Place, Right Plan.*"

—*John Hagee*
Best-selling author
Senior Pastor, Cornerstone Church,
San Antonio, Texas

"As a leader, there are few topics more difficult to navigate than that of discernment. And trying to teach others about it is even more harrowing. But in his book, *Right People, Right Place, Right Plan*, Jentezen Franklin has unveiled the key that unlocks this perplexing subject. Whether you are a leader in the church, business world, education, or home, this book will give you the real-life knowledge you need to hear the voice of God and make the most of your full potential in every situation you face."

—Ed Young
Senior Pastor, Fellowship Church
Author of Outrageous, Contagious Joy

RIGHT PEOPLE, RIGHT PLACE, RIGHT PLAN DEVOTIONAL

RIGHT PEOPLE, RIGHT PLACE, RIGHT PLAN DEVOTIONAL

30 Days of Discerning the Voice of God

JENTEZEN FRANKLIN

WHITAKER
HOUSE

RIGHT PEOPLE, RIGHT PLACE, RIGHT PLAN DEVOTIONAL:
30 Days of Discerning the Voice of God

Jentezen Franklin Ministries
Kingdom Connection
P.O. Box 315, Gainesville, GA 30504
www.jentezenfranklin.org

ISBN-13: 978-1-60374-059-3
ISBN-10: 1-60374-059-7
© 2008 by Jentezen Franklin
Printed in the United States
of America

1030 Hunt Valley Circle
New Kensington, PA 15068
www.whitakerhouse.com

Library of Congress Cataloging-in-Publication Data
Franklin, Jentezen, 1962–
Right people, right place, right plan devotional : 30 days of discerning the voice of God / Jentezen Franklin.
p. cm.
Summary: "Over the course of thirty days, this devotional helps believers develop spiritual discernment in order to make wise life-decisions in accordance with the will of God"—Provided by publisher.
ISBN 978-1-60374-059-3 (hardcover : alk. paper)
1. Discernment (Christian theology)—Meditations. 2. Decision making—Religious aspects—Christianity—Meditations. I. Title.
BV4509.5.F7462 2008
248.4—dc22

2008011015

1 2 3 4 5 6 7 8 9 10 **W** 14 13 12 11 10 09 08

CONTENTS

Days 11–20: Right Place

Days 21–30: Right Plan

INTRODUCTION

How can you discover the unique, internal direction that God has given you? What is God's plan for your life? Many women today can feel anything but special as they try to fulfill the ever-present demands of career, church, and family. They feel left out, stressed out, and frazzled. Most men today are confused as the world tries to feminize them and then expects them to be "real men" by gratifying their every desire. They feel marginalized, emasculated, and under attack.

God sees you as extraordinary, and He desires to use you in extraordinary ways. He is searching for men and women who dare to believe they can make a difference. Today, members of the body of Christ (the church) must open up their spiritual ears to hear and recognize the voice of the Almighty. Could it be that God wants to use you as a key player in His kingdom in these last days?

DEVOTIONAL

First John 2:20 says, *"But you have an anointing from the Holy One, and all of you know the truth"* (NIV). All believers have an anointing—a spiritual touch of God—that provides them with remarkable insight. Through the Holy Spirit, from whom all the gifts, graces, and superior knowledge of God flow, you have inside information on what God's will is. He has given you an internal compass to guide and discern things about your children, your spouse, your family, your career, and your finances.

This discernment is not from human wisdom; it is from God. It is easy to hear God's voice when you are earnestly seeking Him, living within His will, and being edified by spiritually minded friends. Over the next thirty days, we will examine the importance of associating with the right people, being in the right place, and having the right plan. As you will soon see, this will be the most important life lesson you've ever experienced as you fulfill your assignment in becoming the man or woman God created you to be.

Part One:

THE RIGHT PEOPLE

STOP GETTING BURNED

DAY I

There is a friend who sticks closer than a brother.

—Proverbs 18:24

I

STOP GETTING BURNED

Choosing to spend time with the right people is one of the most important decisions you can make in life. It's also one of the most practical areas to begin discerning the voice of God and His will for your life. Have you ever given your best in a relationship but gotten the worst in return? Remember the lyrics of the popular country song, "Lookin' for Love," by Johnny Lee:

> *Lookin' for love in all the wrong places,*
> *Lookin' for love in too many faces.*

That has become a theme song for far too many people.

It's time to put a stop to getting burned. It's time to start enjoying the healthy, balanced relationships everyone wants and needs. God wants to help you make wise choices about the people you let into your life, from friends to business colleagues to spouses. Finding the proper people is an important part of determining God's will for your life. If you have ever been used, abused, abandoned, or taken advantage of in a relationship, this section is for you. Too often, good people get entangled in bad relationships— with disastrous results.

If you start bringing the right voices into your life, you'll begin to make the right choices as well. And once you start making the right choices, you get the right connections. Every time God does something significant in our lives, He introduces us to new people—ones who are connected to our destiny and purpose. Learning to discern God's voice and follow His leading will remove you from bad relationships and bring you into contact with the right people.

I'm going to share how you can hear God's voice and discern His will so that you can distinguish between the "right people" from the wrong people.

Prayer:

Heavenly Father, I pray that over the next thirty days, You will develop the gift of discernment in my life. Guide my thoughts and feelings to mirror Your perfect will for my life. Help me to know the right people from the wrong people and associate with those who are furthering Your kingdom. Amen.

Reflections:

CHARACTER DISCERNMENT

DAY 2

Those who live according to the flesh set their minds on the things of the flesh, but those who live according to the Spirit, the things of the Spirit.

—Romans 8:5

2

Character Discernment

Character discernment is a valuable tool for avoiding toxic entanglements. It is a skill many of us lack. What is character discernment? It is simply the ability to find relationships that are good for you, and to avoid those that are not.

The apostle Paul said, *"You ran well. Who hindered you from obeying the truth?"* (Galatians 5:7). Notice he said *who,* not what. Romans 8:5 says, *"Those who live according to the flesh set their minds on the things of the flesh, but those who live according to the Spirit, the things of the Spirit."*

When some people come into your life, they don't just bring their bodies—they bring their spirits. There are two kinds of people: "flesh people" and "faith people."

Flesh people tear you down and feed your fears, while faith people build you up and feed your faith.

Flesh people waste your time and drain your energy. Often, Christians find themselves in confusing relationships that drain them of their emotional energy and greatly reduce their effectiveness. Think of the personal pain that could be prevented if we knew how to avoid unhealthy relationships.

This doesn't necessarily mean "flesh people" are bad people; it just means they don't belong in your inner circle. It also doesn't mean that you should shun such people; God wants us to love all those we come into contact with. But we have to make sure that we are surrounding ourselves with more people who fill our lives than drain our lives. One of the first warning signs of spiritual failure is when we begin to isolate ourselves from Christian friends and from the house of God.

Faith people are the kind of people who fill your life. They draw you closer to being the person God created you to be. They are the ones who will be lovingly honest with you. They are strong when you are weak.

If God wants to bless you, He will send a person; and if Satan wants to curse you, he will send a person. That's why, every day, we need to pray for 20/20 discernment in the world of the spirit to know the right people from the wrong people.

Prayer:
Father, strengthen me so that I may live according to the Spirit. May your Holy Spirit work within me so that I may be on my guard and accurately discern the things of the flesh from the things of God; the "flesh people" from the "faith people." Please continue to bring supportive "faith people" into my life. In Your holy name I pray, amen.

Reflections:

_____

_____

_____

_____

POWER RELATIONSHIPS

Two are better than one....For if they fall, one will lift up his companion. But woe to him who is alone when he falls, for he has no one to help him up.

—Ecclesiastes 4:9–10

3

POWER RELATIONSHIPS

God wants to release Power Relationships in our lives. The number one reason that people don't get where God desires for them to go, in my opinion, is that they do not know who they're supposed to be around and who they're not supposed to be around. There are three principles that I want to share about Power Relationships.

1. All good things in life flow through relationships. The Bible says that *two are better than one* (Ecclesiastes 4:9).

2. A power connection is God's blessing for transition in your life. In other words, anytime you're about to go to a new level or enter into a new season, God will bring new people into your life. These people—some of them saved, some of them not saved—can become the Power Relationships that release you from the

old and move you into the new season that God has for you.

3. Dormant potential can be unlocked if you enter into Power Relationships. I love this concept because it's the simple truth.

You see, there's a "real you" trying to break out. Power Relationship people are those who speak to that element inside of you and lead you to become the person you've always dreamed that you could be. This can't happen unless you get around a Power Relationship that liberates you from the old patterns, old mess, and old way of thinking that the enemy enslaved you to.

Somebody else is already at the level you're going to. That's a Power Relationship! Somebody else has already made it through the mess you're trying to find your way out of. God has a Power Relationship for you with somebody who's already standing at the place God is leading you to. And that person knows how to reach back down to you; that person knows how to get you from where you are to where you need to be.

All you need to do is ask God for your Power Relationships for the upcoming year, because they've got the information you need.

Prayer:

Lord Jesus, thank You for the Power Relationships that You bring into my life during times of special transition. I ask with confidence and boldness that You will continue to bring these important relationships and connections into my life in the coming year. Use them to unlock dormant potential and lead me into a deeper understanding of Your will and perfect plan for my life. In Your precious name, amen.

Reflections:

_____

_____

_____

_____

PAUL: THE PEOPLE WHO LIFT US UP

God, who comforts the downcast, comforted [me] by the coming of Titus...

—2 Corinthians 7:6

4

PAUL: THE PEOPLE WHO LIFT US UP

The apostle Paul is a wonderful example of a man of God who needed the encouragement and support of other people—the right people that God brought into his life for specific reasons.

When Paul needed to be healed, whom did God send? Ananias was the right man in the right place at the right time. (See Acts 9:10–18.) That's what I call a "Kingdom Connection": people God puts in your life who act like bridges to get you where you're supposed to go. If Ananias hadn't been sent by God, Paul's ministry would have never begun. How would you like some Kingdom Connections in your life and career?

Even after Paul's conversion, the early church rejected him because of the persecution he had waged against Christians before meeting God. The disciples were afraid of him, so God once again sent a person: Barnabas. Barnabas used his influence with the disciples to get Paul's foot in the door of the church:

> *And when Saul had come to Jerusalem, he tried to join the disciples; but they were all afraid of him, and did not believe that he was a disciple. But Barnabas took him and brought him to the apostles. And he declared to them how he had seen the Lord....* (Acts 9:26–27)

Finally, when Paul was discouraged, God sent Titus to encourage him. Have you ever had a discouraging day until one person shared some kind words and completely changed your mood? Even the apostle Paul, who was filled with the Spirit of God, had days like this. In 2 Corinthians 7:6, Paul said, *"God, who comforts the downcast, comforted us by the coming of Titus."*

Prayer:

Lord God, it is encouraging to see how You brought the right people into Paul's life when he was most in need of Your grace. I trust You to do the same for me, because You are the God who never changes and never stops caring about His children. Thank You for the grace and support that You provide through the fellowship of believers on earth. Amen.

Reflections:

_____

_____

_____

_____

_____

_____

RUTH: THE PEOPLE WE MARRY

DAY 5

Praise be to the LORD, who this day has not left you without a kinsman-redeemer.

—Ruth 4:14 (NIV)

5

RUTH: THE PEOPLE WE MARRY

Marriage is one of the most important decisions you will ever make. It is a commitment for life. It affects every other area in your life: your future children, where you live, your finances, where you go to church, and so much more. God has a plan for the people you associate with in your dating life. You will be better off if you take the time to be sure that the one you marry is the one ordained by God.

Does God care if you are single, widowed, or divorced? Does He notice when everybody else goes home together, but you go home alone? You bet He notices! In the book of Ruth, we see the God who said, *"It is not good that man* [or woman] *should be alone"* (Genesis 2:18), step into the shadows of Ruth's life and give her a Kingdom Connection.

Ruth's husband had died, and she had little prospect of finding a good man. But God didn't send her a loser or a reject. He didn't send her a smooth-talking "player" who would break her heart. He sent her a man who was capable and could care for her. He sent her Boaz. Tomorrow we'll perform an in-depth examination of Boaz's character to demonstrate God's unfailing provision.

In the end, Boaz arranged a legal wedding and became Ruth's "*kinsman-redeemer.*" They had a son named Obed. Obed had a son named Jesse. Jesse had a son named David, who became a king. David had a descendant named Mary. And Mary had a little child whom she named Jesus.

Through Ruth's character discernment, God not only blessed her with a fantastic husband, but He also placed her in the genealogy of Jesus Christ. (See Matthew 1:5.)

Prayer:

Heavenly Father, I thank and praise You that You care about all aspects of my life, including the details of my earthly relationships. Through the example of Ruth, I know that You will provide for Your children when they seek Your face with purity of heart. Like Ruth, help me to trust and wait on You as I seek to bring the right people in my life. Amen.

Reflections:

Boaz: The Right Man for Ruth

Then Boaz said to Ruth, "You will listen, my daughter, will you not? Do not go to glean in another field, nor go from here, but stay close by my young women. Let your eyes be on the field which they reap, and go after them. Have I not commanded the young men not to touch you? And when you are thirsty, go to the vessels and drink from what the young men have drawn."

—Ruth 2:8–9

6

BOAZ: THE RIGHT
MAN FOR RUTH

Boaz was a bit older than Ruth, but he had enough money to make her comfortable. Notice the qualities that you should look for, or teach your children to look for, when trying to discern the right mate. Boaz was a stable man. He wasn't just out of prison or rehab. Nor was he lazy and unproductive.

Notice also that he was respectful of Ruth's relatives. He gave Ruth food to take home to her mother-in-law, Naomi. Boaz paid the bill; they didn't "go Dutch." These days, men don't seem to understand how to respect a woman or show respect to her parents. Ladies, if you are dating a guy who reluctantly pays for the meal on the date but expects you to pay for the movie and the popcorn, then you're dating a deadbeat. Take notes here, gentlemen. Boaz was a man's man—a perceptive man, a sensitive man, a spiritual man, and a financially capable man. That's an equation that equals a *husband!*

When Ruth came home loaded with food, Naomi began to teach her how to conduct herself in a proper way. When Ruth wanted to know what she should do about this man showing her romantic interest, Naomi gave her some sound advice: *"Sit still, my daughter, until you know how the matter will turn out"* (Ruth 3:18). "Sit still and wait." In other words, "Let the man pursue you; don't pursue him." Today, the girl would call back in thirty minutes saying, "Do you remember me, Boaz? I met you in the field." The next morning she would be calling again. "Do you remember me? Can we go out on a date sometime?" Men lose respect for desperate women.

Sitting still and waiting is the hardest thing to do. This actually means you will have to trust God in the matter. Even if you're camping out by the phone, waiting on him to call, don't let him know it. Sit still and wait! Ruth could have reacted selfishly and told Naomi, "You don't know what you're talking about. Just because you lost your husband doesn't mean that I'm going to lose a chance at a second one." But she didn't. The Bible says she respected and obeyed Naomi's advice.

Prayer:

Lord Jesus, help me to wait on You, knowing that Your perfect timing is the only catalyst for Your perfect gift. When the going gets tough, bring influential and wise mentors like Naomi into my life to keep me focused on You.
In Your name, amen.

Reflections:

JONAH: THE PEOPLE WHO TAKE US DOWN

DAY 7

*They picked up Jonah and
threw him into the sea, and the
sea ceased from its raging....
Now the LORD had prepared
a great fish to swallow Jonah.
And Jonah was in the belly
of the fish three days
and three nights.*

—Jonah 1:15, 17

7

JONAH: THE PEOPLE WHO TAKE US DOWN

We need God to restore discernment within us so that we can recognize the right people, the blessed people, the faith people, the Kingdom Connections He has for each one of us. But we also need discernment to recognize the wrong people.

God sent Jonah on a mission to Nineveh. But Jonah disobeyed God's will and headed in the opposite direction to Joppa, where he boarded a ship for Tarshish. Many of us have heard the story of Jonah in sermons and Sunday school lessons, but have you ever stopped to consider the fact that there were other people on the boat about to lose their lives besides Jonah? All it takes is one rebellious, disobedient man to take a whole shipload of people down with him.

This is an important lesson for those trying to learn discernment. There are times when you are not the problem. The problem may be the people with whom you're associating. The mariner's boat was taking on water, everyone on board was terrified for their very lives, and it wasn't their fault. They were in the wrong place, at the wrong time, with the wrong person—Jonah.

The Bible says that before they threw Jonah off the boat, they tried rowing harder to bring the ship to land. We often try harder to work on a problem because we are afraid of the decision we know we are going to have to make. Finally someone on the boat called a meeting and decided to throw Jonah off the boat. I'm sure the mariners felt bad about it, but they knew that if they didn't throw him off, they were not going to make it to the other side. As soon as you get the wrong people out of your boat, your storm will cease. Some of you need to throw some Jonahs off your boat!

If you throw a Jonah off your boat, remember that God is still there for him. When the mariners threw Jonah off the boat, God had already prepared a great fish to swallow him and spit him back onto the shore so he could travel on to Nineveh, his intended destination. When you allow the wrong people in your life, you're not helping them—you may be keeping them from what God has prepared for them.

Prayer:
Lord God, give me the discernment to know when I'm not the problem—and the strength, in those situations, to toss the negative influence overboard! Please continue to strengthen my spirit and bring me into contact with people who will support godly decisions.
In Your holy name, amen.

Reflections:

JONAH: THE PEOPLE WHO MAKE US FEEL GUILTY

[Jonah] *said to them, "Pick me up and throw me into the sea; then the sea will become calm for you. For I know that this great tempest is because of me."*

—Jonah 1:12

8

JONAH: THE PEOPLE WHO MAKE US FEEL GUILTY

When the mariners first woke Jonah from his sleep, they asked him, *"What shall we do to you that the sea may be calm for us?"* (Jonah 1:11). Jonah answered, *"Pick me up and throw me into the sea; then the sea will become calm for you. For I know that this great tempest is because of me"* (verse 12). Jonah knew he was the problem. So, why would he ask them to cast him over? Why not just jump off the boat?

Sometimes rebels try to make you feel bad. If you have a forty-five-year-old son who won't get a job, still lives at home, eats your food, and pays no rent, then it's time to throw Jonah off the boat! When you do, don't be surprised if he tries to make you feel guilty for doing the right thing. I can just hear his pitiful words, "You're right; I know I should do better. I'll just find somewhere else to stay. I guess I could sleep at the bus station."

We can wander into storms simply by trying to help people by doing for them what they should be doing for themselves. If the mariners had not tossed Jonah off the boat, everyone would have perished. If you have people in your life who are using you for a free ride, they're not going to voluntarily jump off the boat. If you have relatives or friends who play on your conscience and goodwill to get you to pay their bills or give them money, do you think they're going to stop? If you have a husband who physically abuses you or has affairs on the side and you allow it, you are giving him a license to treat you like a dog.

As soon as Jonah was off the boat, the mariners began to worship God. (See Jonah 1:16.) You cannot worship God as you ought to as long as there are toxic relationships and turmoil all around. Whatever is stealing your peace and rocking your boat, whatever is taking your smile away, reach down, pick it up, and throw it overboard. Then do what the mariners did—start worshipping God.

Prayer:
Heavenly Father, I ask again for the wisdom to know the right people from the wrong people; and when You've shown me the wrong people, keep me safe from the negative effects of guilt. Give me the courage to sever ties with people who have a negative influence on my life, and help me to live purposefully for You. Amen.

Reflections:

WHO'S YOUR MENTOR?

*The things which you learned
and received and heard and saw
in me, these do, and the God of
peace will be with you.*

—Philippians 4:9

9

Who's Your Mentor?

One of the secrets of success for some of the great Bible heroes was having mentors. If you don't have a godly mentor in your life, you need to ask God to put one there. When He does, don't hang back and wait for the person to approach you; you may need to ask him or her to mentor you. Joshua was always there, hanging out around Moses. Elisha's success was found in his relationship with Elijah. He spent hours and hours learning from the wise old prophet.

The apostle Paul called Timothy *"a true son in the faith"* (1 Timothy 1:2). Timothy was one of the youngest apostles in the Bible. How did he succeed at such a young age? He literally sat at the feet of the great apostle Paul and caught his spirit.

Jesus spent three and a half years of His life in ministry. Most of His time was not with the crowds, or with rich and influential leaders, but with twelve men into whom He poured His life and wisdom. He would speak in parables to the crowds of people, then He would explain and elaborate with the disciples. These men became the building blocks of His church.

Mentors expose you to new orbits of ministry, new habits, and new levels of expectation. Ask the weight lifter or the track-and-field high jumper what a coach does for him. If you want to be the best, the mentor will keep raising the bar, asking for a little more effort and for better results, and teaching you to expect more from yourself.

At times, mentors may even seem cruel and inconsiderate, but if you want to be a winner, their coaching can urge you to the top. Proverbs 27:6 says, *"Faithful are the wounds of a friend, but the kisses of an enemy are deceitful."* It's a great day when God gives you someone who loves you enough to put you under a little pressure so you can be conformed into the image of Jesus Christ and reach your highest potential.

Prayer:
*Lord Jesus, thank You for the example of those
who are mature in their faith. I pray not only
that You would bring powerful mentors into my
life, but also that You would keep me humble so
that I can learn from them and follow You more
closely. In Your name I pray, amen.*

Reflections:

BEWARE FALSE BRETHREN

DAY 10

Every branch in Me that does not bear fruit He takes away...

—John 15:2

10

Beware False Brethren

If you have spent your life gravitating toward all the wrong people, I have good news for you. God will bring the right people and toss out the wrong people. But when He does, don't return to the wrong people. *"Every branch in Me that does not bear fruit He takes away"* (John 15:2).

That does not mean they're inferior and you're superior; it just means they are not a part of God's plan for your life. Like Jonah, God has a different plan, a different course, for them. But if you insist on grafting them into your life, God may have to do relational surgery and prune them out.

Unfortunately, such false brethren can sometimes be found within your own family, where it is hard to prune them out. At family gatherings, they often bring condemnation. It was only when the prodigal son failed that he realized what his older brother was made of. Upon his return and repentance, his father did not bring up the sins of the prodigal. It was his elder brother who pointed his finger and condemned the prodigal son to his father. (See Luke 15:11–32.)

Joseph discovered that false brethren never celebrate your dream. Instead of living in God's land of unlimited favor, they live in a "zero sum" mentality where for you to win, they must lose. Your gain is their loss. If you receive blessing, they believe somehow there are fewer blessings available for them. Joseph's brothers couldn't stand their father's favor toward the young lad, so they threw him into a pit and sold him into slavery. (See Genesis 37:24.)

Some people bless you when they come into your life; some people bless you when they exit your life. There are many good people out there. *There is a friend who sticks closer than a brother* (Proverbs 18:24). Use every ounce of wisdom and discernment to find such people. If someone is destructive or producing bad fruit in your life, be careful. Keep looking, praying, and seeking until you find the right people who draw you closer to being the person God intended you to be.

Prayer:
Loving heavenly Father, I pray that You will keep me both vigilant and wise as I interact with others. I ask for the gift of discernment and pray for the strength to use it as You reveal to me the difference between "flesh people" and "faith people." Keep me always close to You, Lord Jesus. Amen.

Reflections:

_____

_____

_____

_____

_____

Part Two:

THE RIGHT PLACE

CANCEL
THE DEVIL'S
ASSIGNMENT

DAY

II

*God has set the members, each
one of them, in the body just as
He pleased.*

—1 Corinthians 12:18

11

Cancel the Devil's Assignment

One of God's primary purposes for your life is proper placement. Being in the right place at the right time is an important key to discovering God's will for your life. In Genesis 1, God created a place and He created Adam; in Genesis 2, God planted Adam into his proper place: the garden.

What does this tell you about God and His will for your life? Two things:

1. God doesn't leave you where He finds you.
2. God has a proper placement for you.

The owner of the first "placement service" in the world was God. Paul wrote, *"God has set the members, each one of them, in the body just as He pleased"* (1 Corinthians 12:18). God comes to you right where you are and gives you a purpose, a mission, and a place. God gave Adam a place of employment before He gave him a wife. If you're a single woman, you shouldn't consider marrying any man who doesn't have his place of employment—a job.

More than twelve years ago, God began to speak to me about this amazing gift of discernment. I had a dream one Saturday night that was so vivid I will never forget it. I dreamed I was attending the funeral of a child. When I walked up to the little casket and looked in, I was devastated to see Caressa, my three-year-old daughter, lying lifeless in the coffin. Immediately, I woke up from the dream and awakened my wife. We both began to pray for our family. We wept as the strong presence of the Lord entered our bedroom.

The next morning, still shaken by this experience, I went to church to preach. I preached a sermon I titled "Cancel the Devil's Assignment." At the end of the message, I tearfully told the congregation about my dream. I explained how I believed God was warning me that Satan had targeted our children at a young age, but through the blood of Jesus Christ, we could cancel the devil's assignment in their lives.

It was one of the most moving services I've ever taken part in, as fathers and mothers began to cry out to God on behalf of their families. Yet God had an even more specific plan in store...

Prayer:

Heavenly Father, thank You that You have a specific place in mind for each of Your children. I ask You for the wisdom to recognize the devil's snares and to stay in tune with Your will for my life. Lead me in the direction that You would have me to go. Amen.

Reflections:

_____

_____

_____

_____

_____

GOD'S PLACEMENT BRINGS HEALING

We do not have a High Priest who cannot sympathize with our weaknesses, but was in all points tempted as we are...

—Hebrews 4:15

12

GOD'S PLACEMENT BRINGS HEALING

This is where the story I began yesterday takes a dramatic turn. Our family had planned to go on vacation to Disney World in Florida the next day after I preached the sermon, but for some strange reason, my wife begged me to leave right after the morning services so we could visit SeaWorld first. We decided to go even though it hadn't been on our itinerary.

While we were there, a sudden storm broke out, and a streak of lightning hit the top of a nearby hotel, setting it on fire. Panic-stricken, five thousand people rushed up the steps of the stadium we were in, seeking shelter from the storm. Total chaos ensued. In the midst of everything, our youngest daughter, Caressa, ran right past her mother to a total stranger standing nearby. The stranger, a twenty-six-year-old woman, reached down and picked her up without hesitation, sobbing uncontrollably as she held our three-year-old daughter.

Worried, we asked the young woman's parents, who were standing nearby, what was going on. "Two months ago, my daughter's three-year-old child died of congestive heart failure in the middle of the night," the woman's mother said. "This is the first time we have been able to get our daughter out of her bedroom because she has been so devastated with grief. She's been blaming God for taking her little girl."

I told the young mother who was holding Caressa about the prophetic dream I had preached on the previous day, and that God had brought us to Sea-World that day to let her know that her precious daughter is with Him in heaven. I went on to tell her that our three-year-old has never run into the arms of a complete stranger. "This is a sign from God to you of how much He loves you," I said. The young woman told us that this experience had restored her faith in God.

If we are hurting, God hurts, too. *"For we do not have a High Priest who cannot sympathize with our weaknesses"* (Hebrews 4:15). Jesus allowed Himself to be forsaken by God so He could say, "I know, I've been there." Our God knows the pain of loss. He is moved by the same things that distress us. Think of it: out of thousands of people at SeaWorld that day, God put us in the right place, at the right time.

Prayer:

Lord Jesus, I am open to Your leading in my life. Take me to the places I need to be for the service and advancement of Your kingdom, and use me to bless others. Keep me open to Your leading. In Your holy name, amen.

Reflections:

_____

_____

_____

_____

YOUR GEOGRAPHICAL PLACE OF DESTINY

From one man he made every nation of men, that they should inhabit the whole earth; and he determined the times set for them and the exact places where they should live.

—Acts 17:26 (NIV)

13

YOUR GEOGRAPHICAL
PLACE OF DESTINY

Destiny is living according to God's plan for your life. You become a person of destiny when you realize that God has a plan for your life and a geographical place of destiny for you and your family. God has a destiny for families; His commitment to our lives is not just for us, but it is multigenerational. God's plan for my family will outlive me; He's doing things now, setting up my children and my grandchildren for His destiny.

Churches also have specific destinies. Genesis chapter 11 tells us that Terah, the father of Abraham, was a man who went halfway. God told him to go all the way to Canaan, but he reached a city called Haran and just settled there. He became relaxed and comfortable, and he made up his mind that it wasn't worth the fight anymore. *I'm halfway to my destiny*, he thought, *but I don't want to go any further than this lush valley.* It was just too comfortable.

I imagine Terah started thinking, *All the bills are paid, and I don't have to pray a lot. I don't have to be under stress. I don't have to use my faith to get what I need. I'm in a comfortable place, and it would be best if my family just stayed and lived here.*

That's where many people are today: they've settled for less. Many of you have gone far and know there's more out there, but something in you is withdrawing and saying, "Well, you'd better not go too far. You'd better just relax. You know you don't need to trust God for more."

But the Lord is saying, "I have new plans for you. I have new opportunities for you. I have new people and new places and new plans that I want to release into this season of your life." If we're not careful, we'll become like Terah. The Bible says that he "*came to Haran and dwelt there....and Terah died in Haran.*" (Genesis 11:31–32). Our lives should be about more than simply living and dying; God has a marvelous plan in store for us if we will only listen and learn to discern His will.

Prayer:

Father in heaven, lead me to my destiny; lead me into Your plan for my life. I am open to Your leading. Give me the strength to reject complacency and avoid becoming settled in the wrong place. In Your name I pray, amen.

Reflections:

GEOGRAPHICAL CHANGE MAY BRING SPIRITUAL PROMOTION

DAY 14

*The LORD had said to Abram,
"Leave your country, your
people and your father's
household and go to the land I
will show you."*

—Genesis 12:1 (NIV)

14

GEOGRAPHICAL CHANGE MAY BRING SPIRITUAL PROMOTION

God knows when it's time to move on, and He admonishes Christians not to get comfortable where they are. In 1 Samuel 16, Samuel was weeping because Saul had lost the kingdom. God came to him and said, *"How long wilt thou mourn for Saul, seeing I have rejected him from reigning over Israel? fill thine horn with oil, and go...for I have provided..."* (1 Samuel 16:1 KJV).

God has provided everything you need to start again. Sometimes we're mourning over what we've lost or some bad episode in our lives. Maybe you lost your job, have been through a divorce, or experienced some other kind of difficult setback. But listen to what the Lord says: "How long will you cry over that bad episode in your life? Go, for I have provided."

There are friends who are just waiting to be a part of your life the moment you decide to live again. There are opportunities, open doors, places of blessing, and resources that are waiting on you to get up and believe that God still has a plan for you—no matter what has happened in your life. It's time to move on. It's time to get up from the comfortable place and the safe place. It's time to use your faith again—and faith is spelled R-I-S-K.

What happened to Abram when God called him to leave the place where his father died? This man was seventy-five years old with a thousand people depending on him, and yet he turned to his wife and said, "It's time for a geographical change in our lives." Most people get so settled and comfortable that they don't want to change anything, but the Lord is saying that often geographical change positions you for supernatural promotion.

Just think of Abraham, Moses, and Joseph! God called all of them to geographical change, but in each case it brought about a significant spiritual promotion. You've got to listen so that you can "hear" the new orders—the new instructions that God has for your life.

Prayer:

Lord God, I pray that You will destroy the fear of risk that is in my heart and replace it with faith in Your son. Keep me open to geographical change as You lead me to the right place and reveal to me more and more of Your exciting plan for my life. Amen.

Reflections:

_____

_____

_____

_____

_____

DAY

15

PROPER PLACEMENT AFFECTS YOUR FUTURE

*"Arise, go to Zarephath...
and dwell there. See, I have
commanded a widow there to
provide for you."*

—1 Kings 17:9

15

PROPER PLACEMENT AFFECTS YOUR FUTURE

Proper placement profoundly affects your future in several ways. We'll use the rest of this section to examine each of them in turn.

The first is that proper placement releases supernatural provision. First Kings 17:3–4 describes such provision:

Get away from here and turn eastward, and hide by the Brook Cherith, which flows into the Jordan. And it will be that you shall drink from the brook, and I have commanded the ravens to feed you there.

During a famine, God gave Elijah clear instruction, saying, in effect, "Go to Cherith. I have commanded the ravens to feed you *there*." God told Elijah that if he moved to the right place, supernatural provision *would* show up. Divine supply follows divine placement. If Elijah had been any other place but the right place, the ravens would not have fed him. God holds your place of supernatural provision—God has a "there" for you!

Just about the time Elijah thought he had God all figured out, suddenly the brook dried up and the ravens stopped bringing food. I once preached a sermon called, "What to Do When the Brook Goes Dry and the Birds Won't Fly!" In it, I explained that the only reason God lets the brook dry up is that He wants to drive you back to your source. We are to seek God's face, not His hand. We want a handout, but God wants a face-off.

Don't fall in love with a method and forget that God is your source. The brook wasn't Elijah's source; God was. We get married to a method, anchored to a memory, but we must be open to change. When the Holy Spirit wants to do a new thing, we have to get away from the old wineskins. In this case, God gave Elijah a new plan: *"Go to Zarephath....I have commanded a widow there to provide for you"* (1 Kings 17:9).

Prayer:

Lord God, I am thankful for the examples of supernatural provision that You have given us in the Bible. I believe that You can and will provide for me today as faithfully as You provided for Your servant Elijah. Help me to rest secure in the knowledge that Your perfect placement will release Your supernatural provision in my life. Amen.

Reflections:

PLACEMENT RELEASES SUPERNATURAL PROVISION

You visit the earth and water it,
You greatly enrich it; the river
of God is full of water; You
provide their grain, for so You
have prepared it.

—Psalm 65:9

16

PLACEMENT RELEASES
SUPERNATURAL PROVISION

My wife has her own contracting company. Through the years, she has had an uncanny ability to make wise financial investments in the area of real estate. Regretfully, I have not always listened to her. Consequently, we've missed some incredible financial blessings. But I've learned that one of my wife's strong points is in business, so I'm glad to take a backseat to her in this area.

Discern the place of blessing for your life. If God says, "I'll bless you 'there,'" and you insist on staying "here," then you're going to miss His provision.

When Ruth was looking for a place of provision, she expressed her desire to her mother-in-law, Naomi. *"Please let me go to the field, and glean heads of grain after him in whose sight I may find favor"* (Ruth

2:2). You don't want to work in just any field. Pray for discernment that will lead you into an occupational field where you will find the favor of your employer. The place God has for you will be a place of influence, favor, and prosperity.

Sometimes, the place God sends you won't appear to be a place of blessing. When Ruth found the right field in which to work, she labored in only a remote corner of it. Later, she was promoted from working in that insignificant corner to marrying the man who owned the entire field! But, her promotion was contingent upon finding the right place of employment.

Are you in the right place, or are you leaning on an old plow, afraid to let go?

In 2 Chronicles 7:12, God said to Solomon, *"I have heard your prayer, and have chosen this place for Myself as a house of sacrifice."* Oh, the potential of a chosen place. If you are in such a place, don't leave it. If you are not, don't stay where you are another day longer than you have to. In Exodus 33:21, God said to Moses, *"Here is a place by Me, and you shall stand on the rock."* There is a place reserved for you by God. If you will move there, God will supernaturally provide all you need to do His will.

Prayer:
Lord Jesus, help me to let go of my comfortable old habits and trust Your leading in my life. I realize that I will miss Your provision by staying "here" when You have promised to bless me "there." Help me to serve and honor You in all that I do. Amen.

Reflections:

_____

_____

_____

_____

_____

PLACEMENT WITHOUT PRIDE IS PROTECTION

Then Peter got down out of the boat, walked on the water and came toward Jesus. But when he saw the wind, he was afraid and, beginning to sink, cried out, "Lord, save me!"

—Matthew 14:29–30 (NIV)

17

PLACEMENT WITHOUT PRIDE IS PROTECTION

A wrong place is any place where you know your Christian walk is compromised. When you stay out of the wrong places, you protect your integrity. Any place that Christ Himself would not go is the wrong environment. A good rule to follow is, "If Christ wouldn't, you shouldn't!"

In the cool of the day, Adam and Eve would walk with God in the garden of Eden. When they were with God, Satan never showed up. He approached Eve when she was absent from God's presence. As long as Peter stayed near Jesus' side, he was strong in faith; but when he was alone—absent from the presence of Jesus—he warmed his hands by the wrong fire and denied Christ three times. (See John 18:17–18, 25–27.) There is protection in His presence. Don't stray too far from the body of Christ, which is the church, or you'll become easy prey for the enemy.

In order to be completely safe, however, proper placement also demands the death of pride. This is a tough one! Pride is one of the main obstacles blocking your move to the right place. When we are puffed up with pride, we say things like, "Well, I'm not going to work there. I'm better than they are."

Elijah was a great and mighty man of God. He was a big, strong prophet who killed four hundred fifty prophets of Baal and called down fire from heaven. But in 1 Kings, God instructed him to seek help at the home of a widow: *"I have commanded a widow there to provide for you"* (1 Kings 17:9). This would have been a perfect time for pride to swell within Elijah. He could have said, "I'm not going to lower myself by asking for help from that woman." But he didn't allow pride to keep him from the right place.

Men can learn a lot from their wives, but pride won't let them say, "I was wrong; you were right."

Often, finding your proper placement demands the death of personal pride.

Prayer:

Lord Jesus, thank You that Your placement offers me protection as I walk in Your perfect will. Keep me alert and give me the spiritual strength to avoid the sin of pride, which compromises this protection. Keep me close to You, Father. Amen.

Reflections:

PLACEMENT MAY BRING DISCOMFORT BUT HALTS TEMPTATION

DAY 18

"These things I have spoken to you, that in Me you may have peace. In the world you will have tribulation; but be of good cheer, I have overcome the world."

—John 16:33

18

PLACEMENT MAY BRING DISCOMFORT BUT HALTS TEMPTATION

First, proper placement is often preceded by a season of discomfort. The reason is simple: until your misery factor exceeds your fear factor, you won't change. We prize security.

When a mother eagle wants her eaglets to learn how to fly, she begins to tear up the nest. She removes the animal fur to expose the briars and thorns. Suddenly, the nest isn't such a comfortable place anymore, so the eaglets swiftly desire to stretch their wings and learn to soar. You'll never fly if you're too comfortable. You will never change that which you are willing to tolerate. God has a way of making us move out. It's called discomfort.

The good news is that even when our external circumstances may be uncomfortable, Christ Himself has promised to be our internal, spiritual source of undiminishing comfort:

> *These things I have spoken to you, that in Me you may have peace. In the world you will have tribulation; but be of good cheer, I have overcome the world.* (John 16:33)

Second, proper placement prevents exposure to sinful situations and temptations, which will ultimately lead to more discomfort than what you may be experiencing now! If you will listen to and obey God's voice, His glory will be your reward. Failing to do so may subject you to sinful situations and temptations.

The first words God spoke to Adam after he sinned referred to Adam's location. *"Then the LORD God called to Adam and said to him, 'Where are you?'"* (Genesis 3:9). Adam's sin drove him out of the place specifically prepared for him.

Lot was the nephew of Abram, but he left his uncle and moved to Sodom. What was he doing living in Sodom? Lot saw an opportunity to get rich, but eventually he lost his wife in the process because he wasn't where he was supposed to be.

Prayer:
Father, I know that I will have challenges and temptations in this world, even while I am led into the place that You have for me. Help me to trust in You during this time and depend on you to give me the strength to overcome temptation, knowing that You have gone before me and have overcome the world. Amen.

Reflections:

PLACEMENT
RELEASES THE
GLORY OF GOD

*When Moses came down from
Mount Sinai…he was not
aware that his face was radiant
because he had spoken
with the LORD.*

—Exodus 34:29 (NIV)

19

PLACEMENT RELEASES THE GLORY OF GOD

Proper placement releases the glory of God on your life. In the book of Exodus, God told Moses how to construct the tabernacle:

> *I have put wisdom in the hearts of all who are gifted artisans, that they may make all that I have commanded you: the tabernacle of meeting, the ark of the Testimony and the mercy seat that is on it, and all the furniture of the tabernacle; the table and its utensils, the pure gold lampstand with all its utensils, the altar of incense, the altar of burnt offering with all its utensils, and the laver and its base; the garments of ministry, the holy garments for Aaron the priest and the garments of his sons, to minister as priests, and the anointing oil and sweet incense for the holy place.* (Exodus 31:6–11)

Right Place

God gave specific dimensions, colors, and furniture placement, and even specified the garments that were to be worn there. The priests did exactly what God said, and the results were spectacular. *"Then the cloud covered the tabernacle of meeting, and the glory of the LORD filled the tabernacle"* (Exodus 40:34). In 2 Chronicles, after Solomon completed the more permanent temple and all the furniture was properly placed, the Scripture says, *"Fire came down from heaven and consumed the burnt offering and the sacrifices; and the glory of the LORD filled the temple"* (2 Chronicles 7:1). The right place and the right job release the glory of God upon our lives.

Likewise, our very lives can release the glory of God when we live according to His will. All that is required to do this is the willingness to go where God wants to send you. The word *hineni* in the Old Testament was used three times. It means "here am I." Abraham said it; Isaac said it; Isaiah said it. There's a right place for you, but you have to say, "Hineni." Say, "Here am I, Lord. Send me; use me for Your glory. Do something in my life!" God will hear and answer everyone who calls out to Him, and He will show you the place where you need to be to display His matchless glory to the world.

Prayer:

Holy God, I praise You for the opportunity to reflect Your holy glory to the world. Continue to refine me and guide me as I come into the place where I will be best suited for Your service. In Your beautiful name I pray, amen.

Reflections:

_____

_____

_____

_____

_____

PLACEMENT CAN HELP YOU AVOID FUTURE PROBLEMS

*Do not be conformed to this
world, but be transformed by
the renewing of your mind, that
you may prove what is that good
and acceptable and perfect
will of God.*

—Romans 12:2

20

PLACEMENT CAN HELP YOU
AVOID FUTURE PROBLEMS

Living within the proper placement of God can make all the difference between a life of blessing and a life of sorrow. If you live in the right city, go to the right church, find the right job, hang out with the right people, and marry the right spouse, many potential problems will be averted. How do you discover the right place? Repent, pray, and expect divine guidance.

1. Repent; stop doing your own thing.

Psalm 92:13 says, *"Those who are planted in the house of the LORD shall flourish in the courts of our God."* Don't be a tumbleweed Christian, fruitless and rootless, blowing in and out of churches. Get rooted and grounded in the right church. The prodigal son finally came to his senses and realized that he was in the wrong place, living in a pigpen, when he said,

"I will arise and go to my father" (Luke 15:18). He was saying, in effect, "I'm leaving the wrong place and going back to the right place." (See verses 11–32.)

2. Pray for God's timing and God's place.

We are not asking for something that God doesn't know. Acts 17:26 says, *"And He has made from one blood every nation of men to dwell on all the face of the earth, and has determined their preappointed times and the boundaries of their dwellings."* According to Scripture, God assigns a place for you and sets a time for you to be there.

3. Expect divine guidance.

"The steps of a good man are ordered by the Lord" (Psalm 37:23). Missing God's will produces severe consequences. It is my belief that you are safer fighting in a war within the will of God than spending a day at the beach outside of the will of God. Learn to listen to your inner voice of discernment in order to release supernatural provision into your life and the lives of those you meet.

God has a "SeaWorld" assignment for you. Someone out there is in his or her dark night of the soul.

People are counting on you to be sensitive enough to God's leading that you will be in the right place at the right time so He can use you to shine His light into their darkness.

Prayer:

Lord Jesus, give me the strength to stop following my own will and wait for Your guidance to the right place. Give me the faith to expect that guidance, and the courage to pursue Your will when You reveal it to me. I trust You for the future, holy Father. Amen.

Reflections:

Part Three:

THE RIGHT PLAN

GOD'S PERFECT PLAN

DAY 21

*For I know the thoughts that
I think toward you, says the
LORD, thoughts of peace and not
of evil, to give you a future and
a hope.*

—Jeremiah 29:11

21

GOD'S PERFECT PLAN

There is a right plan. One idea from God can change your life. Thomas Edison had one idea, and today we have the electric lightbulb. The Wright brothers had one idea, and now we have aviation. Bill Gates had one idea, and today we have the personal computer. There are "good ideas," and there are "God ideas." The Holy Spirit wants you to discern the difference between the two.

The good news is that God has a plan. You may not know what He's planning for you, but God is a planner! He never does anything by accident. He even has a plan through all of life's tragedies. He's been planning the Marriage Supper of the Lamb for two thousand years. You can be sure He's got a plan for your life. I don't believe that God wants anyone to float around in life.

John the Baptist's mother was told the plan for his life before she was even pregnant. Samson's mother, Manoah, was also told what her boy would be like, the lifestyle he would live, and the plan of God for his life—before he was even born! God has a plan for our lives, our families, our children, and our ministries. And God's plan is ultimately to bring us blessings.

God blesses us in natural ways, but every once in a while, He sends wonderful supernatural blessings into our lives! His plan is perfect, and when we pray, he often leads us to it in awesome, supernatural ways.

Prayer:

Heavenly Father, thank You that You have a plan for my life. This assurance gives meaning to my existence. Please guide me into the knowledge of Your will, and continually reveal to me the parts of Your plan that I'm not aware of yet. Thank You for Your unfailing love and provision. Amen.

Devotional

Reflections:

GET A PLAN

DAY

22

*Love the LORD your God,
walk in all His ways, keep His
commandments, hold fast to
Him, and serve Him with all
your heart and with all
your soul.*

—Joshua 22:5

22

GET A PLAN

Perhaps today you need a miracle for you or your family. When you ask God for a miracle, He will often give you a set of instructions—a plan. He rarely releases a miracle without a plan. Too often we pray and then sit back and wait for God to perform miracles. If you read your Bible, however, you'll find it doesn't work that way. You want a miracle? You're going to receive a set of instructions—a plan.

When Joshua needed a miracle of conquest, God gave him a plan.

You shall march around the city, all you men of war; you shall go all around the city once. This you shall do six days. And seven priests shall bear seven trumpets of rams' horns before the ark. But the seventh day you shall march around the city seven times, and the priests shall blow the trumpets. It shall come to pass, when they make a long blast with the ram's horn, and when you hear the sound of the trumpet, that all the people shall shout with a great shout; then the wall of the city will fall down flat. And the people shall go up every man straight before him. (Joshua 6:3–5)

God said, in effect, "Here's the plan: march six times over six days, and on the seventh day, march seven times. Then blow the horns and shout—and the walls will fall." Joshua obeyed, and God's plan brought down the walls of Jericho.

When Naaman sought a miracle of healing for his leprosy, God provided a plan through the prophet Elisha. *"Go and wash in the Jordan seven times, and your flesh shall be restored to you, and you shall be clean"* (2 Kings 5:10). That simple set of instructions from God brought a miraculous healing to Naaman's body. (See verse 14.)

Before Samson was born, God appeared to his mother and said, *"Behold, you shall conceive and bear a son. And no razor shall come upon his head, for the child shall be a Nazirite to God from the womb; and he shall begin to deliver Israel out of the hand of the Philistines"* (Judges 13:5). God already had a miraculous and detailed plan for Samson's life before the boy was even born.

Prayer:
Lord Jesus, keep my heart sensitive and open to receiving Your instructions, and give me the courage to walk in Your will when You reveal Your plan to me. Amen.

Reflections:

_____

_____

_____

_____

_____

PRAY FOR A MIRACLE

DAY 23

*Therefore I say to you, whatever
things you ask when you pray,
believe that you receive them,
and you will have them.*

—Mark 11:24

23

PRAY FOR A MIRACLE

God didn't just have a plan for His Old Testament servants like Joshua and Sampson; exciting stories of miraculous plans are also found in the New Testament. In the first chapter of Luke, for example, Elizabeth and Zacharias were told by the angel of God that they would have a son. Very little was left to chance.

> *Your wife Elizabeth will bear you a son, and you shall call his name John. And you will have joy and gladness, and many will rejoice at his birth. For he will be great in the sight of the Lord, and shall drink neither wine nor strong drink. He will also be filled with the Holy Spirit, even from his mother's womb. And he will turn many of the children of Israel to the Lord their God. He will also go before Him in the spirit and power of Elijah, "to turn the hearts of the fathers to the*

children," and the disobedient to the wisdom of the just, to make ready a people prepared for the Lord. (Luke 1:13–17)

Once again, the plan of God came with a name and an assignment, before Elizabeth was even pregnant with John the Baptist, their miracle child.

At the wedding in Cana, when Mary asked her Son for a miracle of provision, Jesus gave a plan. Mary had enough experience with the plans of God that she knew what to do.

His mother said to the servants, "Whatever He says to you, do it." Now there were set there six waterpots of stone, according to the manner of purification of the Jews, containing twenty or thirty gallons apiece. Jesus said to them, "Fill the waterpots with water." And they filled them up to the brim. And He said to them, "Draw some out now, and take it to the master of the feast." And they took it. (John 2:5–8)

The water blushed in the presence of its Creator, turning into wine of the highest caliber. (See

John 2:8–10.) When you ask God for a miracle, He connects your miracle result to a miracle plan.

Prayer:
Lord God, throughout history You have answered the prayers of those who have boldly prayed for miracles. Please strengthen my faith and lead me into the knowledge of Your plan so that I too will be able to do great things for Your kingdom. Amen.

Reflections:

_____

_____

_____

_____

_____

KNOW THE SOURCE

DAY 24

Before I formed you in the womb I knew you; before you were born I sanctified you; I ordained you a prophet to the nations.

—Jeremiah 1:5

24

KNOW THE SOURCE

Jeremiah 29:11 says, *"For I know the thoughts that I think toward you, says the LORD, thoughts of peace and not of evil, to give you a future and a hope."* God made you for a purpose. When you don't know why something is made, you can easily abuse it. Don't ask the creation what its purpose is; ask its Creator.

Some of you may be thinking, *You don't know where I came from, the things I've done. You don't know my parents. I came from an illegitimate background.* That doesn't matter to God. Here's what you need to understand: *"Before I formed you in the womb I knew you; before you were born I sanctified you; I ordained you"* (Jeremiah 1:5). You don't come from a background. You don't come from your parents. You may have come *through* them, but you didn't come *from* them. You come from God. Your assignment can't be messed up by your circumstances.

Ephesians 2:10 reminds us, *"For we are His work-manship, created in Christ Jesus for good works, which God prepared beforehand that we should walk in them."* When you were created, God encoded you for an assignment, and He gave you the power to get it done. The enemy's job is to pull us out of that divine assignment, out of the will of God.

The good news is that God has the "inside information" on our lives. First John 2:20 says, *"But you have an anointing from the Holy One, and you know all things."* Do you have questions in your mind? Do you wonder whom you should marry? Do you wonder what you should do with your life? Do you wonder if you should make that investment? *"You have an anointing from the Holy One, and you know all things."*

This means that you can know things you were never educated for. You can tap into a resource, an information source called the Holy Spirit, and you can know things that are beyond your natural education or ability to know. The Holy Spirit is smarter than any human being on earth, and through Him, you can *"know all things."*

Prayer:

Father, thank You for the marvelous assurance that through Your Holy Spirit, I can "know all things"! Help me not to take this gift for granted. Help me to cultivate it through an active relationship with You and a desire to serve You in all that I do. In Your precious and holy name I pray, amen.

Reflections:

GOD'S ROAD MAP TO YOUR PURPOSE

Eye has not seen, nor ear heard,
nor have entered into the heart
of man the things which
God has prepared for those
who love Him.

—1 Corinthians 2:9

25

GOD'S ROAD MAP TO YOUR PURPOSE

Every assignment has a birthplace. Destiny is reached by discerning those transitional moments when God sends you His road map leading to your purpose.

The church where I pastor, Free Chapel, has been in existence for more than fifty years. The former pastor, Roy Wellborn, scheduled me to come preach a revival every year when I was a full-time evangelist. The last time I preached for Pastor Wellborn, it was scheduled nine months in advance. Just prior to the date, however, he became ill, was hospitalized, and passed away. He died on Friday night; I was to preach that Sunday.

The congregation loved Pastor Wellborn. They were devastated at his passing. You can imagine how inadequate I felt standing in the pulpit two days after his death—the pulpit this beloved man had faithfully filled for more than thirty years. As soon as the morning's service ended, they rolled in the coffin and held Pastor Wellborn's memorial service.

At that time, I had no idea that I was there by the divine plan of almighty God. I'm sure that when Pastor Wellborn scheduled me to preach in his church, he had no idea he would be in heaven that very week, or that God had already chosen me as his replacement.

God really does have a marvelous plan for our lives. Pray for special insight into His plans for your life. You will discover that *"eye has not seen, nor ear heard, nor have entered into the heart of man the things which God has prepared for those who love Him"* (1 Corinthians 2:9).

Prayer:
Father God, give me the faith to trust in Your plan, even if I cannot see the evidence of it right

*now. Your Word declares that no eye has seen
what You have "prepared for those who love
[You]," but I know that my final destination is
with You in heaven. Thank You for this hope.
Give me patience and faith along the way.
Amen.*

Reflections:

GOD'S UNEXPECTED PLAN

DAY 26

Esther also was taken to the king's palace, into the care of Hegai the custodian of the women. Now the young woman pleased him, and she obtained his favor; so he readily gave beauty preparations to her, besides her allowance. Then seven choice maidservants were provided for her from the king's palace, and he moved her and her maidservants to the best place in the house of the women.

—Esther 2:8–9

26

GOD'S UNEXPECTED PLAN

God's plan for your life will often come through unexpected events that force you in a direction you never would have gone. Esther experienced the providential leading of God that gave her assignment a "birthplace."

The book of Esther opens with a wild seven-day party in the king's palace. As the icing on the cake, the custom was to bring the queen out to dance in order to close the deal. There was nothing unusual about the king asking Queen Vashti to dance; what was unusual was for her to refuse. When the queen failed to appear, one of his warlords exclaimed,

> *The queen's behavior will become known to all women, so that they will despise their husbands in their eyes, when they report, "King Ahasuerus commanded Queen Vashti to be brought in before him, but she did not come." This very day*

the noble ladies of Persia and Media will say to
all the king's officials that they have heard of the
behavior of the queen. Thus there will be exces-
sive contempt and wrath. (Esther 1:17–18)

Greatly embarrassed, King Ahasuerus decided to get rid of his queen and find a new one via a "national beauty contest." As a result, one hundred twenty-seven women were selected from the provinces for the king's consideration. Esther, a young orphan girl, was chosen as one of them.

Queen Vashti's fatal attitude set the stage for the higher purpose of God. Sometimes, when things happen you can't explain, these paradoxical occurrences tell us that somebody else is in charge. As Christians, we don't believe things in our lives happen by chance; instead, we believe God has a plan for each of us. It's interesting how God often seems to use people with disadvantaged backgrounds—Esther was an orphan. But God has a habit of picking up nobodies and making them somebodies.

Overnight, God placed the orphan girl, Esther, in the palace. Her godly uncle, Mordecai, had raised her and groomed her for greatness. She knew she was special even if she didn't have pretty shoes and even if she lived in a little hut. Mordecai had taught her about her covenant relationship with God.

Prayer:

Lord God, thank You that You enjoy making nobodies into somebodies, and that Your wisdom exceeds and confounds the wisdom of this world. Please guide me to the right place and make me part of Your exciting plan. Amen.

Reflections:

_____

_____

_____

_____

_____

God's Plan Is Greater than We Know

DAY 27

"Who knows whether you have come to the kingdom for such a time as this?"

—Esther 4:14

27

GOD'S PLAN IS GREATER
than WE KNOW

Many times, like Esther, we are oblivious to God's plan for our lives. She probably dreamed of raising a traditional Jewish family, leading an ordinary life, not knowing she was meant for extraordinary things. I'm sure she dreamed of holding hands with her fiancé under the olive tree and planning her wedding ceremony. While she was planning everyday things, God was planning supernatural opportunities for her.

While we are so busy grabbing lesser things, ordinary things, mediocre things, God is planning extraordinary things for our future. Don't let anyone tell you that you can't reach for the stars. Even if you don't get there today, you possess the potential that promises, maybe tomorrow, you will make it.

"We know that all things work together for good to those who love God, to those who are the called according to His purpose" (Romans 8:28).

A godly man laid the groundwork in Esther's childhood to prepare her for her life assignment. When the king selected his new queen, out of all those women, he chose Esther.

Esther had been groomed, psychologically and spiritually, to become great. God often sets a mentor alongside to give insight, wisdom, and direction. Esther had Mordecai, Ruth had Naomi, and Mary had Elizabeth. Timothy had the faith of his mother and grandmother. Paul wrote, *"I call to remembrance the genuine faith that is in you, which dwelt first in your grandmother Lois and your mother Eunice, and I am persuaded is in you also"* (2 Timothy 1:5).

You could be your children's mentor. What you speak into your children's lives today may prepare them for unexpected greatness and unlimited opportunities.

Prayer:

Lord Jesus, thank You for the mentors You have brought into my life—the people who have helped me gain wisdom and reach the place where I am right now. As I grow in faith, use me to bless others in similar ways, revealing to them that Your plan is always bigger than they think. In Your powerful name I pray, amen.

Reflections:

GOD'S PLAN
PURIFIES US

*Therefore, having these
promises, beloved, let us cleanse
ourselves from all filthiness of
the flesh and spirit, perfecting
holiness in the fear of God.*

—2 Corinthians 7:1

28

GOD'S PLAN PURIFIES US

God had a purpose for young Esther higher than being the king's contest winner. Before this young girl was selected from her province to enter the contest, she didn't know proper protocol: she hadn't been taught formal table manners; she didn't know how to curtsy; she didn't know the right clothes to wear; she didn't display manners befitting royalty. Yet, God selected this ignorant orphan girl, fresh from the hills. Like Cinderella, her foot "fit the glass slipper," and she found favor with the king.

The king chose Esther not because she was Jewish or because he had a spiritual revelation. He was simply using his senses, unaware that God was guiding his eyes. Did you know that God is able to use people who aren't spiritual? Have you ever had someone say to you, "I don't know why I'm doing this for you; I don't know why I'm breaking the rules for you"? They're telling the truth—they don't know why they're helping you. They can't explain intelligently why they want to help you. God will even use your enemies to make a way for you when you're in His will. Proverbs 16:7 says, *"When a man's ways please the LORD, He makes even his enemies to be at peace with him."*

Once Esther was in the palace, she had to go through a purification process. Along with the call of God comes "the process." We like to be called out and chosen by God, but for every calling there is a discipline.

First, Esther had to bathe in oil for six months. In Scripture, oil signifies the Holy Spirit. This woman was going to determine the fate of her nation. She had to be anointed. She was affecting future generations. Queen Vashti was an independent woman concerned with doing her own thing, but Esther understood it was not about her thing; it was about following God's plan.

Men, sometimes your friends will make fun of you for being spiritually minded. They may mock your sensitivity and compassion while tempting you to revert back to your cold, detached, self-reliant past. Ask yourself, *How is that working out for my so-called "friends"?* Remember that it takes more courage and machismo to remain sensitive to the things of God than it does to run from Him and live life on your own.

Prayer:

Lord Jesus, You know that God's plan is not always comfortable and fun. As a human, I know that I must be continually purified as I seek to follow Your will. Please give me the strength and spiritual endurance to run the race well, and further Your kingdom purposes. Amen.

Reflections:

_____

_____

_____

_____

THE POWER
OF PRAISE

*Therefore by Him let us
continually offer the sacrifice of
praise to God, that is, the fruit
of our lips, giving thanks
to His name.*

—Hebrews 13:15

29

THE POWER OF PRAISE

The second step of Esther's purification process was being perfumed. You know what perfume does. It makes you smell nice; it draws people to you. In the Bible, incense represents people's praise to God. There was an altar of incense in the Old Testament tabernacle. When the priest poured the perfume on the hot coals of the altar of incense, the scent would go up to heaven. The Bible says that God received the incense offering as a sweet-smelling savor of praise. (See Leviticus 2:2.)

Of course, under the new covenant, we don't have to sprinkle incense on a fire. All we have to do is open up our mouths and give God the fruit of our lips, which is the fragrance of praise in His nostrils. (See Hebrews 13:15.)

When we praise God verbally, it's like spraying the most expensive perfume or cologne; it goes up to heaven and creates an aroma that gets God's attention. Praise is more than making a noise. When you praise Him, you invite the presence of God, the calm of God, and the serenity of God into your life.

Praise is called "the oil of myrrh." Remember the wise men who came to Bethlehem when Jesus was born? They brought frankincense and myrrh, which denote praise and adoration. Learn to be a worshipper.

Esther's scent reached the king before she did. The reason the king extended his scepter to Esther was that she filled the throne room with her perfume of praise before she was given access into the king's presence. We, too, come into God's presence first by the aroma of our praise.

No wonder the ultimate worshipper, the psalmist David, said, *"Enter into His gates with thanksgiving, and into His courts with praise. Be thankful to Him, and bless His name"* (Psalm 100:4). Esther was chosen, groomed, oiled, and perfumed.

When you praise, you get a sense of what God wants you to do. With praise comes prophecy. With praise comes direction. With praise comes God's plan for your life.

Prayer:

Lord God, how could I think of You and fail to praise Your name? Forgive me for the times when praise has not flowed readily from my lips. You are truly worthy of all adoration and praise, and I want to make my life a constant, fragrant sacrifice to You. Amen.

Reflections:

_____

_____

_____

_____

_____

DON'T FORGET THE PLAN

You therefore, beloved, since you know this beforehand, beware lest you also fall from your own steadfastness, being led away with the error of the wicked; but grow in the grace and knowledge of our Lord and Savior Jesus Christ.

—2 Peter 3:17–18

30

DON'T FORGET THE PLAN

I'm sure that after six months of bubble baths, massages, pedicures, manicures, pampering, the opulence of the palace, and the luxurious lifestyle Esther was afforded, she began to dull a little spiritually. If you are not careful, you may become so spiritually pampered and comfortable that you will forget there is a godly reason for being where you are. This is no time to get comfortable! There is still a plot to annihilate our children, our homes, our marriages, and our nation. You have a call of God upon your life; you have an appointment with destiny.

While Esther got comfortable and almost forgot her purpose, Mordecai put on sackcloth. (See Esther 4:1.) Sackcloth is ugly-looking clothing. He got ugly. Every now and then, we have to "get ugly" to get God's attention. We have to afflict ourselves with fasting and prayer. Mordecai reminded Esther that she was not just there to look good and to wear beautiful clothing. No, there was a mission!

> *Do not think in your heart that you will escape in the king's palace any more than all the other Jews. For if you remain completely silent at this time, relief and deliverance will arise for the Jews from another place, but you and your father's house will perish. Yet who knows whether you have come to the kingdom for such a time as this?* (Esther 4:13–14)

Don't forget your purpose. To all of you Esthers out there—men and women—know that there is a plot to destroy your family. We all enjoy being pampered, but there is a battle to fight and a victory to win. There is a cause! Be anointed with the oil of the Holy Spirit; be perfumed with passionate praise for God. You have come to the kingdom for such a time as this. Jesus prayed, *"Not My will, but Yours, be done"* (Luke 22:42). Pray and expect God to give you the right plan for your life.

Prayer:

Heavenly Father, I pray now, at the conclusion of this thirty-day journey, that You will give me the right plan for my life. Lead me into Your will, Father. Guide me according to Your purposes. Not my will, but Yours be done. Help me to love, honor, and serve You in all that I do. Bring me into contact with the right people, in the right places, and in accordance with Your perfect and everlasting plan. In Your holy name I pray, amen.

Reflections:

_____

_____

_____

_____

_____

CONCLUSION

I hope that you have been edified by the thoughts and reflections that I have shared over the past thirty days. By now you should know with complete assurance that God's will is readily available to those who are with the right people, in the right place, and with the right plan. I trust and pray that you are developing the essential gift of discernment as you strive to bring these three elements into focus.

Stay open to divine interruptions. When God does a new thing, it's not like the old thing. Lot's wife only appears one time in the Old Testament. Why did Jesus tell us to remember her? (See Luke 17:32.) It was because she refused to break with her past. She turned into a lifeless monument. Stop rehearsing your beginning, and write the rest of your story. In Isaiah, God even told His prophet, *"Behold, I will do a new thing, now it shall spring forth"* (Isaiah 43:19).

If you're afraid of the future, remember that God has never failed you. May He bless you powerfully.

Final Reflections:

About the Author

Jentezen Franklin is the pastor of Free Chapel in Gainesville, Georgia, with a congregation of ten thousand in weekly attendance. Named as one of the top thirty churches in America by *Outreach Magazine*, Free Chapel has recently grown into a new location in Orange County, California, where Pastor Franklin also speaks weekly.

Through his experience as a pastor, teacher, musician, and author, Pastor Franklin seeks to help people encounter God through inspired worship and relevant application of the Word of God in their daily lives. His national television program, *Kingdom Connection*, is seen in prime time weekly on various national and international networks.

Pastor Franklin is a popular speaker at numerous conferences across the country and around the world. He has also written several books, including the best-selling *Right People, Right Place, Right Plan* and the *New York Times* best-seller *Fasting: Opening the door to a deeper, more intimate, more powerful relationship with God.*

Franklin and his wife, Cherise, live in Gainesville with their five wonderful children.

Right People, Right Place, Right Plan:
Discerning the Voice of God
Jentezen Franklin

Whom should I marry? What will I do with my life?
Do I take this job? Should I invest money in this opportunity?

God has bestowed an incredible gift in the heart of every
believer. He has given you an internal compass to help
guide your life, your family, your children, your finances,
and much more. Jentezen Franklin reveals how, through the
Holy Spirit, you can connect with the heart and mind of the
Almighty. Learn to trust those divine "nudges" and separate
God's voice from all other voices in your life. Tap into your
supernatural gift of spiritual discernment, and you will better
be able to fulfill your purpose as a child of God.

ISBN: 978-0-88368-276-0 • Hardcover • 208 pages

www.whitakerhouse.com

A Deeper Level
Israel Houghton

Grammy Award-winning artist and worship leader, Israel Houghton invites you to venture with him and his band, New Breed, to *A Deeper Level*. While journeying with them, you will discover that worship is much more than singing songs and going to church. As you go deeper, you will find yourself able to live in the constant presence of God, to differentiate between character and anointing, and to break destructive attitudes of ego and pride.

God is moving and calling this generation to make a kingdom difference in our world.
Dive in…and go deep!

ISBN: 978-0-88368-804-5 • Trade • 160 pages

WHITAKER HOUSE

www.whitakerhouse.com